Lao Tzu's Tao Te Ching
老子之　道 德 經

The Way of Nature
and
The Way of People

English

First Edition

Dr. Auke Schade

nemonik-thinking.org

Copyright

First Edition
Published August 20, 2016
@ nemonik-thinking.org
ISBN 978-0-473-37078-7

Abstract

This is an abridged version of *Lao Zi's Dao De Jing (Schade, 2016)*, which means—*The Way of Nature and the Way of People*.[1] Lao Zi was a Chinese philosopher who lived during the 6th century BC but is still ahead of our time. His brilliance outshines intellectual giants such as Confucius, Sun Zi, Socrates, Plato, and Aristotle. Lao Zi's aim is to teach success, which is to *obtain what you seek and escape what you suffer*. Success is achieved by aligning the *Way of People* with the *Way of Nature*. Lao Zi's success is secular and based on competence, rather than devotion. It is about positioning, rather than competing. Lao Zi's deep understanding of nature and people is crucial for your immediate survival and that of the next generation. We are facing overpopulation, dwindling resources, nuclear warfare, pollution, climate change, etc. We cannot solve those problems with the same way of thinking that is causing them. The brutal reality shows that our way of thinking is failing. Therefore, Lao Zi's eternal wisdom is the guiding light for our future. Its simplicity reaches peacefully across the boundaries of race, religion, spiritualism, ideology, and science.

---

[1] The different titles are the result of alternative spellings.

Dr. Auke Schade

My life started during the devastation of World War II. As a teenager, I worked as a carpenter and studied building engineering at night school. During the seventies, I became a financial manager for a multinational corporation, ran my own business, and studied economics in my spare time. My interest in the psychology of management extended to the interaction between the mind, body, and reality. In 1980, I immigrated to New Zealand where I obtained a doctorate in psychology from the University of Auckland. My mission is to make people the smartest thinkers they can be, which has led me to the development of nemonik thinking.[2]

Download free eBooks and videos
@ nemonik-thinking.org

---

2 Appendix: Nemonik Thinking

Notes

Content

Introduction

Lao Zi (6th cent. BC) explains in one clear sentence the simple purpose of his allegedly mysterious *Dao De Jing—Use it to obtain what you seek and to escape what you suffer (62).* His inspirational guideline provides a sophisticated yet simple principle for success.

Apparently, Lao Zi's biography was written down by the historian Ssu-ma Ch'ien (145-90 BC) who compiled the first comprehensive history of China. Nevertheless, mystery still surrounds the person of Lao Zi. Even his name is ambiguous. It could mean either *old boy* or *old father.* Some scholars suggest that Lao Zi was born with white hair and therefore was called *old boy.* On the other hand, *old father* might refer to a kind of honorary title such as *elder* or *old master.* Lao Zi's real name might have been Li Erh, who was a historian in the state of Chu.

Legend has it that Lao Zi left Chu because of the unbridled corruption in that state. Travelling through a narrow mountain pass, the keeper of that pass asked him to write down his wisdom. Allegedly, Lao Zi wrote *Dao De Jing* in one might. It might be that the pass refers to the change from life to death and that he wrote the manuscript during the last days of his life.

Dao De Jing might be a compilation of older ideas, because Lao Zi refers to the *Ancients* as his source of wisdom. However, we might say the same about any textbook of modern science. All those books show that in the past many scientists have contributed to the knowledge we have today. The only difference is that modern scientists have adopted the custom of mentioning the source of the ideas. Although honourable, that custom does not make knowledge any more reliable or valid.

The possibility that many scholars have contributed to *Dao De Jing* does not reduce the value of either the author or his manuscript. Although similar aphorisms might have been widely known at that time, *Dao De Jing* provides a consistent theory about the origin, formation, and working of the Universe. It is unlikely that such a sophisticated theory would appear accidentally from a compilation of unrelated sayings.

Dao means literally—*road, path, way, or pathway*. However, most scholars agree that in the context of Lao Zi's philosophy, *Dao* means—*The Way of Nature* or simply—*The Way*. The Way is the origin, principle, substance, and force of the Universe. On the other hand, *De* could be translated as—*The Way of People*. Furthermore, *Jing* denotes that scholars consider Lao Zi's manuscript a classic book. Thus, we could translate *Dao De Jing* as—*A Classic about the Way of Nature and the Way of People*.

It is hard to overestimate Lao Zi's wisdom and insight. He explains how to become a sage and use the inexhaustible forces of nature to your advantage. Sages are competent people who align with the *Way of Nature*. For that reason, they aim continuously to be in the right place, at the right time, with the right resources and in the right frame of mind.

Many wise people including Aristotle, Buddha, and Confucius have emphasized that moderation is the key to lasting success. However, only Lao Zi explains clearly why that is inevitably the case.

Right now, humanity's conventional way of thinking is failing, because it reinforces winning, rather than success. That leads to counterproductive criticism, rationalization, cognitive dissonance, and groupthink. As a result, we are facing manmade global problems such as overpopulation, dwindling resources, industrial pollution, insane warfare, and cold-hearted social-economic inequality. Yesterday's solutions have become today's problems. We cannot hope to solve those problems with the same way of thinking that has created them. Therefore, the eternal wisdom of Lao Zi's *Dao De Jing* is more relevant than ever.

Lao Zi's Dao De Jing
老子之　　道 德 經

The Way of Nature
and
The Way of People

道

Dao

The Way of Nature

Chapters 1—37

1

The Way that can be discussed is not the eternal Way. The name that can be named is not the eternal name. Nameless it is the origin of All-things. Being named it is the Mother of All-things. Therefore, be always without desire and see the details. Have always desires and see the limits. These two things occur together. Different names with the same meaning. Profoundly mysterious, they are the gateway to many details.

2

If everyone in the world recognises beauty as beautiful, then there is already ugliness. If everyone recognizes good as goodness, then there is already badness. Therefore, Existence and Non-existence generate each other. Difficult and easy turn into each other. Long and short shape each other. High and low fill each other. Tone and voice harmonise each other. Before and after follow each other forever. Therefore, sages manage their affairs with Non-action. They carry out their teachings without speaking. All-things rise, but do not initiate them. Act, but do not rely on it. Succeed, but do not claim. Only that what is not claimed can therefore not be taken away.

3

Do not promote the knowledgeable and the people will not strive. Do not admire goods that are difficult to obtain and the people will not steal. Do not display what is desirable and the people will not revolt. Therefore, sages rule by emptying the minds of people, filling their stomachs, weakening their ambitions, and strengthening their bones. Let the people be always without knowledge and without desire. Let those who know, not dare to act but stop. Act with Non-action, then there will be no anarchy.

4

The Way is empty, but use it and it has not to be refilled. It is so deep! Like the ancestor of All-things: it smooths their blending, untangles their disorder, softens their glare, and merges their dust. Invisible. Nevertheless, it seems to exist. I do not know whose child it is, but it seems to predate the Emperor.

5

The Sky and the Earth are not benevolent, because All-things act as straw dogs. Sages are not benevolent, because common people act as straw dogs. What is between the Sky and the Earth is like a bagpipe. It is empty, but not exhausted. Use it and more will be produced. Listening to many details is exhausting and not as good as following your heart.

6

The immortal Valley Spirit is called the Mysterious Female. The home of this Mysterious Female is called the origin of the Sky and the Earth. It seems to exist forever and using it is no hard work.

7

The Sky endures and the Earth last long. Why do the Sky and the Earth last long and endure? That is, because they do not foster themselves. Therefore, they can live long. Accordingly, sages withdraw themselves. Yet they are first. They put themselves outside. Yet they are inside. Because they are selfless, therefore, their self-interest is fulfilled.

8

Superior goodness is like water. The goodness of water benefits All-things and it does not strive. It occupies places everybody dislikes. Therefore, it is close to the Way. In dwelling, the goodness is location. In thinking, the goodness is depth. In giving, the goodness is benevolence. In speaking, the goodness is truth. In ruling, the goodness is order. In working, the goodness is skill. In action, the goodness is timing. Only those who do not strive will therefore not fail.

9

Accumulating and filling up is not as good as stopping in time. Hammer it too sharp and it cannot last long. A room filled with gold and jade cannot be defended competently. Admiring wealth and arrogance brings personal loss and misfortune. When merit is achieved, withdrawing yourself is the Way of nature.

10

Carry the 'corps de esprit' and unite it inseparable with the One. Concentrate vital energy and be as soft as an infant. Study and eliminate mysteries. Inspect them competently without flaws. Love the people and rule the country without using knowledge. Open and close the gates of nature as a female. Understand the surroundings without using knowledge. Generate them and raise them. Generate but do not possess. Develop but do not exploit. This is called profound virtue.

11

Thirty spokes merge into one hub, but its Non-existence is useful for a carriage. Moulded clay makes a cup, but the Non-existence of clay is useful for a cup. Chiselled doors and windows make a room, but their Non-existence is useful for a room. Therefore, using Existence is beneficial, while using Non-existence is useful.

12

The five colours will blind people's eyes. The five tones will deafen people's ears. The five flavours will refresh people's mouth. Galloping and hunting in the field will overexcite people's minds. Goods that are difficult to obtain will harm people. Therefore, sages will rule for the stomach and not for the eyes. Therefore, reject that and accept this.

13

Favour and disgrace are just like distress. They cause great suffering just like the body. Why saying that favour and disgrace are just like distress? Favour is inferior. Receiving it is like distress and losing it is like distress. Whether it is called favour or disgrace, it is like distress. Why saying that it cost great suffering just like the body? Why do I have great suffering? That is, because I have a body. If I had no body, how could I suffer? Therefore, those who purposely value their body for serving the world can be entrusted with the purpose of the world. Those who purposely love their body for the world can be entrusted with the world.

14

Look at it, yet it cannot be seen. Its name is called invisible. Listen to it, yet it cannot be heard. Its name is called inaudible. Seize it, yet it cannot be caught. Its name is called insubstantial. These three phenomena cannot be extensively evaluated, because they merge into the One. Above the One there is no void. Below it there is no substance. It is infinite. It cannot be named. Every time it returns to nothing. It is called shapeless. Like the shape of nothing. It is called dim and elusive. Face it, yet you do not see its head. Follow it, yet you do not see its back. Adhere to the present Way in order to manage the present Existence. Use it to understand its ancient origin. That is called the principle of the Way.

15

Those Ancients who practised the Way competently, understood profoundly the smallest details. Their depth cannot be known. They cannot be understood. Therefore, they are difficult to describe and called: "Careful, like they were wading through a river in the winter. Hesitant, like they were afraid of their surrounding neighbours. Solemn, like they were guests. Dissipating, like they were melting snow. Vague, like they were simple. Empty, like they were a valley. Merging, like they were mud." Do not stir mud and it will slowly clear. If settled, stir it and then it will slowly come alive. Those who keep the Way do not desire fullness. Only those who desire no fullness are therefore able to exhaust themselves without renewal.

16

Concentrate on removing extremes. Nurse tranquillity faithfully. All-things around us rise, and I watch them return. Those things are numerous and each one returns to its roots. Returning to the roots is called tranquillity. Tranquillity is called returning to order. Returning to order is a constant. Knowing this constant is brilliant. Not acknowledging this constant is arrogant. Arrogance causes misfortune. Knowing this constant is embracing. Embracing is honourable. Honourable is Kingly. Kingly is natural. Natural is the Way. The Way is forever. It provides a content life without danger.

17

Great leaders are those known by their subjects to exist. Next are those that are loved and praised. Next are those that are feared. Next are those low ones who are insulting. If there is not enough trust, then there is distrust. Those of value speak about their plans and succeed in completing their affairs. Yet, the common people will say; it happened naturally.

18

Therefore, if the great Way is rejected, then there will be benevolence and justice. Knowledge and cleverness will appear and then there is great hypocrisy. Family relationships will be disharmonious and then there is animal dirt everywhere. The State's household will be a confused disorder and then there is bureaucracy.

19

Discard adoration and reject knowledge and the people will benefit a hundred times. Discard benevolence and reject righteousness and the people will return to filial piety and compassion. Discard cleverness and reject profit and there will be no burglars and thieves. These three declarations could be regarded to be inadequate slogans. Therefore, let the people have also institutions. Show modesty and embrace simplicity. Lack selfishness and restrain desires.

20

Discard knowledge and there are no worries. Flattery and rebuke: how much do they differ from each other? Satisfaction and dissatisfaction: how much do they differ from each other? What everybody fears, one has to fear as well. Everybody stares at me. They do not stop. Everybody is very happy. Just like a big sacrificial feast in the village and stepping on stage in the springtime. I am quiet and not predictable. Just like a baby that has not coughed yet. Tired; without a place to return to. Everybody has a surplus. Yet, only I seem to be lacking. I am a very stupid fool in other people's minds. Everybody is very clear. Only I seem to be confused. Everybody is very certain. Only I seem to be very uncertain. They are indifferent. It is like staring at the sea. It is like having no place to rest. Everybody has a purpose. Only I am stubborn and my purpose seems to be ridiculous. Only I desire to differ from other people and value the food from the Mother.

21

The greatest virtue is following only the Way. The contents of the Way are only elusive and dim. Dim. Elusive. Inside there are images. Elusive. Dim. Inside there are things. Tranquil. Obscure. Its centre has energy. Its energy is very real. Inside it, there is information. From past to present times, its name was never erased. Therefore, align with the Father of the Multitude. How do I know that the Father of the multitude is like this? From this account.

22

Bend then be preserved. Twist then be straightened. Empty then be filled. Exhaust then be renewed. Lack then receive. Have surplus then be confused. Therefore, sages hold on to the One. Accordingly, they are the shepherds of the world. They do not display themselves. Therefore, they are brilliant. They do not regard themselves. Therefore, they are honoured. They do not boast about themselves. Therefore, they have merit. They are not arrogant. Therefore, they will develop. They do not strive. Therefore, no one can strive with them.

The ones called the 'Ancients' said: *"Those who bend will be preserved."* Is that saying insignificant? However, true preservation was their return.

23

Speaking seldom is natural. Violent storms do not drum all morning. Violent rains do not drum all day. Who serves them? The Sky and the Earth. Yet, they cannot go on forever. So how about people? Therefore, those who submit their affairs to the Way will merge with the Way. Those who submit their affairs to virtue will merge with virtue. Those who submit their affairs to loss will merge with loss. Those who merge with virtue will also gain the Way. Those who merge with loss will also lose the Way.

24

Those who stand on tiptoe do not stand firm. Those who display themselves are without brilliance. Those who regard themselves are without honour. Those who boast about themselves are without merit. Those who are arrogant are without development. Their Way is called: *"Leftover food and unnecessary action."* These things are disgusting. Therefore, those who have desires will not succeed.

25

There was a thing undivided and complete before the Sky and the Earth were born. Desolate. Empty. Independent and unchanging. Yet, it acts as the origin of the world. I do not know how its name is pronounced, but I call it the Way. If I were forced to name it, then I would call it great. Great means continuous. Continuous means forever. Forever means returning. Therefore, the Way is great. The Sky is great. The Earth is great. The King is also great. Inside the Universe there are four Greatnesses and the King is one. Therefore, people follow the Earth, the Earth follows the Sky, the Sky follows the Way, and the Way follows nature.

26

Heaviness is the foundation of lightness. Tranquillity is the sovereign of rashness. Therefore, great men who travel all day will not leave their heavy wagons. Although, there is a walled guest house in a quiet place nearby, they remain aloof. Just like a lord with ten thousand chariots who considers himself less important than the State. Lightness will lose the foundation. Rashness will lose the sovereign.

27

Competent travellers leave no trail. Competent speakers pursue no flaws. Competent accountants do not use bamboo counting sticks. Competent wardens lock without keys. Yet, it cannot be opened. Competent weavers arrange without strings. Yet, it cannot be untied. Therefore, sages save people always competently by not rejecting them. Not rejected things are resources. Accordingly, that is called brilliant. Therefore, competent people are the teachers of incompetent people. Incompetent people are the resources of competent people. Those who do not value their teachers, or do not love their resources, although knowledgeable, are greatly confused. This is called the essential detail.

28

Know the male and guard the female and become the stream of the world. Be the stream of the world and the eternal virtue never leaves. If the eternal virtue never leaves, then you will return to infancy. Know the white and guard the black and be the example for the world. Be the example for the world and the eternal virtue never errs. If the eternal virtue never errs, then it returns to moderation. Know the pure and guard the disgrace and be the valley of the world. Be the valley of the world and the eternal virtue will always be enough. If the eternal virtue is always enough, then you will return to simplicity. Simplicity breaks up and then it becomes tools. Sages use them and become official leaders. They will not divide great organisations.

29

If anyone would desire to take the world and interfere with it, I see that they have no alternative. The world is a container of energy that cannot be interfered with. Those who interfere will fail. Those who hold will lose. Things may succeed or may fail. They may be hot or may be cold. They may be strong or may be weak. They may grow or may decay. Therefore, sages reject extremes, reject grandeur, and reject extravagance.

30

Use the Way to assist the leaders of people. Do not use soldiers to force the world. Such actions are likely to rebound. Where armies have camped only thorny bushes will grow. Those who are competent succeed and stop in time. Do not dare to take power. Succeed without boasting. Succeed without attacking. Succeed without arrogance. Succeed without excess. That is called succeeding without force. Strong things will become weak. They are not called the Way. What is not the Way will soon perish.

31

Armies are the tools of misfortune. They are disgusting. Therefore, those who possess the Way will not claim them. Great men will occupy and value the unorthodox. They will use soldiers who value the orthodox. Armies are the tools of misfortune. Therefore, armies are not the tools of great men. When there is no alternative then use them. Attack with sharp weapons to become victorious, but use them without satisfaction. Those who are satisfied by it, like to kill people. Those who like to kill people cannot achieve the goals of the State. Therefore, during fortunate events, the left side is honoured. During funerals, the right side is honoured. Therefore, junior generals occupy the left side, while senior generals occupy the right side. Their places are determined in accord with funeral ceremonies. If people were killed, then many will attend with sadness. Hence, treat battle victories as funeral ceremonies.

32

The Way is forever nameless. It is so simple. Yet, the world should not dare to control it. If Marquises and Kings would follow it, then All-things would submit themselves. If the Sky and the Earth would unite with each other, then it would rain sweet dew. People would not have to be ordered, but they would balance themselves. If an organisation is established names will appear. If names appear, then know that it is time to stop. Know when to stop and there will be no danger. The Way is to the world, what a valley is to a river, and what a river is to the sea.

33

Those who know other people are wise. Those who know themselves are brilliant. Those who overcome other people have power. Those who overcome themselves are strong. Those who know what is enough are rich. Those who are strong pioneers have ambition. Those who do not lose their institutions will last long. Those who die, but are not forgotten, will live on.

34

The Way floats. It can be unorthodox or orthodox. It completes its affairs successfully. Yet, it is not a famous being. All-things return to it. Yet, it does not act as their master. It is always without desire. Hence, it could be named small. All-things return to it. Yet, it does not act as their master. Hence, it could be named great. Therefore, sages can achieve greatness, because they do not act great. Therefore, they can achieve greatness.

35

Hold on to the great image, and the world will come. It will come without harm and with great calm. Music and food will stop passing travellers. However, words describing the Way are called: bland and without taste. Look at it, and there is not enough to see. Listen to it, and there is not enough to hear. However, use it and it cannot be depleted.

36

To fold something, it must have been unfolded before. To weaken something, it must have been strengthened before. To abandon something, it must have been attached before. To seize something, it must have been separated before. This is called profound brilliance. The soft and weak will overcome the strong. A fish should not leave the deep water. The sharp weapons of the State should not be used in view of the people.

37

The Way is forever nameless. If Marquises and Kings could follow it, then All-things would transform themselves. If this transformation would cause desire, then I would suppress it by using the simplicity of the nameless. Suppressing it by using the simplicity of the nameless will not disgrace them. Use tranquillity without disgrace and the world will regulate itself.

德

De

The Way of People

Chapters 38—81

38

Superior virtue pursues no virtue. Therefore, it is virtue. Inferior virtue pursues virtue. Therefore, it is no virtue. Superior virtue uses Non-action and there is no action used. Superior benevolence acts and yet there is no use in those actions. Superior justice acts and there is purpose in those actions. Superior propriety acts and if there is no agreement, then the arms are bared. Therefore, after the Way is lost there will be virtue. After virtue is lost, there will be benevolence. After benevolence is lost, there will be justice. After justice is lost, there will be propriety. Those who have propriety possess only a thin layer of loyalty and sincerity, which is the beginning of disorder. Those who pretend to know the future are the fruitless flowers of the Way and the chiefs of fools. Therefore, great men occupy the thick and do not occupy the thin. Occupy the fruit, but do not occupy the fruitless flowers. Therefore, reject that and accept this.

39

Of those in the past that obtained the One: the Sky obtained the One through pureness; the Earth obtained the One through quietness; the mind obtained the One through effectiveness; the valley obtained the One through filling; and Marquises and Kings obtained the One by regulating the world. The conclusion about the One is: if the Sky is not clear yet, then fear that it will crack; if the Earth is not quiet yet, then fear that it will burst; if the mind is not effective yet, then fear that it will cease; and if the valley is not full yet, then fear that it will be dry. All-things grow without purpose. If Marquises and Kings do not use superior nobility, then fear that they will be overthrown. Therefore, the noble must use the ignoble as their foundation. The high must use the low as their foundation. Therefore, Marquises and Kings call themselves unkindly 'orphans and widowers'. They use that ignobility incorrectly as their foundation. Therefore, they give too much honour without honour. Hence, do not desire the great splendour of jade, but the grace of natural rock.

40

Returning is the movement of the Way. Weakness is used by the Way. The world's things originate from Existence. Existence originates from Non-existence.

41

If competent scholars hear about the Way, then they are able to practise it constantly. If mediocre scholars hear about the Way, then they put it in a safe place and seem to lose it. If incompetent scholars hear about the Way, then they laugh loudly about it. If they did not laugh loudly about it, then they could practice the Way. Therefore, an established saying states: *"The bright Way seems to be obscure, the Way forward seems to be backwards, and the smooth Way seems to be rough."* Superior virtue is just like a valley. Great pureness seems to be disgrace. Extensive virtue seems to be insufficient. Established virtue seems to drift along. Plain truth seems to change; the greatest square is without edges; the greatest talent matures late; the greatest sound is a rare tone; and the greatest form is without shape. The hidden Way is nameless. Yet, only the Way is good at the beginning and good at the end.

42

The Way generated the One. The One generated the Two. The Two generated the Three. The Three generated All-things. All-things carry Yin on their back and carry Yang in their arms. Their balance creates vital energy that restores harmony. People dislike being unrelated orphans and widowers. Yet, Kings and Marquises use those names for themselves. Things may be harmed by benefit and may benefit by being harmed. Therefore, the teachers of humanity discus and teach people that violent people will achieve nothing but death. I will use that as the father of my teachings.

43

The softest of the world will overcome the hardest of the world. What is without substance will penetrate what is without gaps. Therefore, I know that there is benefit in Non-action. Teaching without speaking and Non-action will benefit the whole world. Only a few competent people can attain this.

44

Fame or life? What is closer? Life or wealth? What is worth more? Gain or loss? What hurts more? Most people love to spend a lot. The larger their hoard the more they have to lose. Therefore, know what is enough and there will be no disgrace. Know when to stop and there will be no danger. Accordingly, one will endure long.

45

The greatest achievement seems to be incomplete. Yet, its usefulness is not reduced. The greatest fullness seems to be empty. Yet, its usefulness is never exhausted. The greatest straightness seems to bend. The greatest skill seems clumsy. The greatest triumph seems insufficient. Activity overcomes the cold. Tranquillity overcomes the heat. Hence, pure tranquillity can be used to regulate the world.

46

If the world possesses the Way, then race horses will be kept for their manure. If the world is without the Way, then war horses will be bred in the suburbs. No greater suffering than having extreme desires. No greater misfortune than not knowing what is enough. No misfortune is more disastrous than the desire to accumulate. Therefore, know that enough is enough and there will be always enough.

47

Do not leave home in order to learn about the world. Do not look through the window in order to learn about the Way of nature. The more that people travel far away the less they know. Therefore, sages do not travel and yet they know. They do not see and yet they name. They do not act and yet they achieve.

48

Those who daily pursue knowledge will expand. Those who daily pursue the Way will contract. Contract and contract until there is Non-action left. There is Non-action and yet there is action. If one wants to take the world, then one should always use no effort. When effort is needed, then there is never enough to take the world.

49

Sages are always without opinions. They use the opinions of common people as their opinions. They are good to those who are good. They are also good to those who are bad. So they gain goodness. They trust those who trust them. They also trust those who do not trust them. So they gain trustworthiness. Sages depend on the world. Careful, so that they become merged with the opinion of the world. All common people focus their ears and eyes. Instead, all sages are like children.

50

Emerging into life is entering into death. Three in ten are companions of life. Three in ten are companions of death. Three in ten people live extremely and move into the realm of death. What is the reason? That is because they live extremely. They are incompetent in hiding, listening, and conserving their lives. Do not walk through the hills in order to meet rhinoceroses and tigers. Do not join the army in order to carry weapons. Rhinoceroses have no place to ram their horns. Tigers have no place to strike their claws. Soldiers have no place to thrust their swords. What is the reason? Because sages avoid the realm of death.

51

The Way generates them and virtue raises them. The environment shapes them and competence completes them. Therefore, All-things respect the Way and admire virtue. Respecting the Way and admiring virtue is not done to obtain a noble position, but it is always done to be natural. The Way generates them and raises them. It grows them and satisfies them. It straightens them and matures them. It supports them and repairs them. Generate but do not possess. Act but do not rely on it. Grow but do not exploit. This is called profound virtue.

52

The beginning of the world is the Mother of the world. Obtain the Mother in order to know her children. When knowing her children, return to their nursing Mother, and life will not be in danger. Block the exchange and close the doors; and to the end of life there will be no hard work. Open the exchange and meddle in affairs; and to the end of life there will be no safety. To perceive the small is called brilliant. Following the soft is called strength. Use its light to join its brilliance again. Not losing life to disaster is called following the constant.

53

Let me have pure knowledge. When walking on the Great Road, the only thing I fear is action. The Great Road is very smooth. Yet, people prefer the narrow winding roads. Their palaces are very clean. Their fields are overgrown with weeds. Their storehouses are very empty. Those who wear embroidered coloured silk, carry sharp swords, gorge on food, and have a surplus of goods and resources, are called 'boasting thieves'. Boasting thieves are not the Way.

54

Those who establish it competently cannot be pulled away. Those who embrace it competently cannot be separated. Accordingly, descendants will pay homage forever. Cultivate it in yourself and it will be genuine. Cultivate it in your household and it will be plenty. Cultivate it in your village and its virtue will last long. Cultivate it in your country and its virtue will be abundant. Cultivate it in the world and its virtue will be extensive. Use yourself to examine yourself. Use households to examine households. Use villages to examine villages. Use countries to examine countries. Use the world to examine the world. How do I know that the world is like this? From this account.

55

Those who have substantial virtue could be compared to new-born babies. Scorpions, vipers, and insects do not bite them. Birds of prey will not seize them. Their bones are weak and their tendons soft. Yet, their grip is firm. They do not know about the joining of male and female. Yet, their male organ is vigorous. Their energy is optimal. They cry all day. Yet, they do not become hoarse. Their harmony is optimal. Knowing harmony is called the constant. Knowing the constant is called brilliance. Benefiting life is called fortune. Using the mind's vital energy is called powerful. Strong things will become weak. They are not called the Way. What is not the Way will perish soon.

56

Those who know do not speak. Those who speak do not know. Block the exchange and close the doors. File their sharpness. Untangle their disorder. Soften their glare. Merge their dust. This is called profound unification. It cannot be achieved by attachment. Neither can it be achieved by detachment. It cannot be achieved by benefit. Neither can it be achieved by harm. It cannot be achieved by admiration. Also, it cannot be achieved by contempt. Therefore, the world admires it.

57

Use justice when ruling the State. Use surprise when employing armies. Use no effort when taking the world. How do I know it is like this? Only after this. The more prohibitions there are in the world, the poorer the people will be. The more sharp weapons people have, the more the State's household will be confused. The more people know, the stranger the things they begin to develop. Rules increase the content of the law and, therefore, there will be more criminals. Hence, the saying of the sages states: *"I practice Non-action and the people will transform themselves. I am tranquil and the people will perfect themselves. I use no effort and the people will become wealthy by themselves. I desire not to desire and the people will become simple by themselves."*

58

If the laws are very lax, then the people will have extreme surpluses. If the laws are very strict, then the people will have extreme shortages and misfortune. Misfortune is fortune's place to hide. Fortune is misfortune's place to hide. Who knows their extremes? There is no normal. Normal turns around and becomes abnormal. Good turns around and becomes evil. That has confused everybody for a long time. Therefore, sages are interfering but not cutting, sharp but not stabbing, straight but not rigid, and bright but not dazzling.

59

In ruling people and working with nature there is nothing like frugality. Only those who are frugal are called to early service. Prepare for the call to serve early by a significant accumulation of virtue. If there is a significant accumulation of virtue, then nothing is impossible. If° nothing is impossible, then one's limits are unknown. If one's limits are unknown, then one may possess the country. Possess the Mother of the country and accordingly endure long. That is called: having deep roots and a strong foundation. Having a long life through a lasting regard for the Way.

60

Ruling a large country is like enjoying small delicacies. Use the Way to attend to the world, then spirits will have no power. It is not that spirits have no power, but their power will not harm people. Not that power cannot harm people. Sages do not harm people either. Both do not harm each other. Therefore, virtue unites and returns.

61

A large country should take a low position. It is the intersection of the world. It is the female of the world. The female always uses tranquillity to overcome the male. She is tranquil. Therefore, she is better in a low position. Hence, a large country should use a lower position than a small country, when associating with that smaller country. A small country should use a lower position than a large country, when associating with that larger country. Therefore, some might take the lower position to associate. Others might be in the lower position to associate. Those in a large country only desire to merge and raise people. Those in a small country only desire to join other business people. They all obtain what they desire. Therefore, the larger one better acts as the lowest one.

62

People and All-things concentrate on the Way. It is the protection for competent people. It is the sanctuary for incompetent people. Pleasing words might be exchanged. Respectful conduct might honour people. Incompetent people forsake their existence unnecessarily. Therefore, when the Emperor is crowned and the three ministers are installed, a mill-stone of jade preceded by four horses, is not as good as sitting down and presenting this. So, why did the Ancients value the protection of this Way? Did they not say: *"Use it to obtain what you seek and use it to escape what you suffer."* Therefore, it is valuable for the whole world.

63

Act with Non-action. Work without effort. Taste without savouring. Make the large small and the many few. Repay hatred with kindness. Pursue the difficult, while it is easy. Act large, while it is still small. The world's most difficult things arise from the most easy ones. The world's largest things arise from the smallest ones. Therefore, all sages will avoid great actions. Hence, they can achieve greatness. Those who make rash promises are certainly difficult to trust. Those who regard everything as easy will have certainly many difficulties. Therefore, sages regard everything as difficult. Hence, they have no difficulties in the end.

64

That what is at rest is easy to hold. That what is not manifest is easy to plan. That what is fragile is easy to break. That what is small is easy to scatter. Act when it has not happened yet. Control it when it is not chaotic yet. A tree that takes both arms to embrace grows from a little cutting. Nine-tenth of a tower rises from a simple basket of earth. A thousand meters height starts from under your feet. Those who act will fail. Those who hold will lose. Therefore, sages will use Non-action. Therefore, they will not fail. They will not hold. Therefore, they will not lose. In handling their affairs, people fail often close to their success. Therefore, be as careful at the end as at the beginning. Then affairs will not fail. Therefore, sages desire not to desire and do not admire goods that are difficult to obtain. They learn not to learn and repair the mistakes of others. Sages complement the nature of all All-things, but they do not dare to act.

65

Therefore, the Ancients said: *"Do not use the Way to enlighten people."* Instead, use it to keep them simple. People are difficult to rule if they use their knowledge. Therefore, using knowledge to rule the country is betraying the country. Using no knowledge to rule the country is benefiting the country. Remember always those two things. Examine also the principle. Always remembering to examine the principle is called profound virtue. Profound virtue is deep. Even far away things return to it. The great order is perfect.

66

How are the river and the sea able to be the Kings of a hundred valleys? They use competently their low position. Therefore, they are able to be Kings of a hundred valleys. Therefore, sages who desire to be above the people must place themselves below them. Those who desire to lead people must place themselves behind them. Therefore, they stay above and the people will not weight them down. They stay in front and the people will not harm them. Everyone in the world will be happy to elect them without objection. Having no purpose, they do not strive. Therefore the world cannot strive with them.

67

Everyone in the world calls me great. Great and different. Only those who are different can be great. If they were similar, then they would be insignificant. I have always three treasures that I keep and protect. The first one is called compassion. The second one is called frugality. The third one is called humbleness. Those who are compassionate can be courageous. Those who are frugal can be generous. Those who do not dare to act as the first of the world can be successful leaders of affairs. Now, those who abandon compassion and are yet courageous; abandon their frugality and are yet generous; abandon their humbleness and are yet leading; they will certainly die. Those who use compassion to attack will triumph. Those who use it to defend will stand firm. Nature will protect them with a wall of compassion.

68

Competent warriors do not like war. Competent chiefs will not get angry. Competent conquerors will not engage. Competent leaders will take a low position. That is called the virtue of not striving. That is called employing people. That is called matching with nature. It is the ultimate principle of the Ancients.

69

Warriors have a saying that states: *"I do not dare to act as a host, but act as a guest. I do not dare to advance an inch, but retreat a foot."* That is called: moving without moving. Rolling up the sleeves without showing an arm. Be without resistance. Hold without weapons. No greater misfortune than meeting no resistance. Meeting no resistance is close to losing my treasures. Therefore, when equal armies face each other the reluctant one will win.

70

My words are very easy to understand and very easy to apply. Yet, people cannot understand them and they cannot apply them. My words have precedence and my affairs have a sovereign, but they do not understand that. Therefore, they do not understand me. I am valuable to those few who understand me. Therefore, sages wear cheap cloth and conceal jade.

71

Knowing that you do not know earns respect. Not knowing that you do not know is a weakness. Therefore, sages are not weak. They consider their weakness as a weakness. Hence, it is not a weakness.

72

When people do not fear authority, then greater authority will appear. Do not take their dwellings by force. Do not reject them a place to live. Only, if they are not rejected, then they will not reject you. Therefore, sages know themselves, but do not display themselves. They love themselves, but do not admire themselves. Therefore, reject that and accept this.

73

Those who are courageous in daring will be killed. Those who are courageous in not daring will live. Those two things could be beneficial or could be harmful. Nature takes a low place. Who knows its reason? The Way of nature is not to strive, but to overcome through competence. Without speaking, it answers with competence. Without calling, things come. It is simple and plans with competence. The net of nature is very extensive. It dredges and nothing escapes.

74

If people never fear death, how could the use of executions scare them? If people always fear death and act abnormal, how could I dare to seize, hold, and execute them? If people always fear certain death, then there is always someone in charge of executing them. Those who act on behalf of the one that is in charge of the executions, execute as if they act on behalf of the Master Carpenter. From those who act on behalf of the Master Carpenter only a few will not cut their hands.

75

People are hungry, because their food taxes are high. Therefore, they are hungry. Common people cannot be governed, because their leaders act for their own purposes. Therefore, the people cannot be governed. People take death lightly, because they seek to live substantially. Therefore, they take death lightly. Only those who do not act for the purpose of living are knowledgeable at valuing life.

76

People are born soft and weak. They die, hard and strong. All-things, grasses, and trees are born soft and fragile. They die, dry and brittle. Therefore, the hard and strong are called companions of death. The soft and weak are the companions of life. Hence, a strong army will not win. A strong tree will be broken. Therefore, the strong and big occupy the low positions. The soft and weak occupy the high positions.

77

The Way of nature is like flexing a bow. High things are lowered. Low things are raised. It takes from those who have plenty. It gives to those who have not enough. Therefore, it is the Way of nature to take from what is plenty and give to what is not enough. However, the Way of people is different. They take from what is not enough and give to what is plenty. Hence, those who have plenty and give to those in the world who have not enough are the only ones who possess the Way. Therefore, sages act, but do not rely on it. They succeed, but do not claim. They do not desire to display their knowledge.

78

Nothing in the world is as soft and weak as water. Yet, in attacking hard and strong things, nothing has a greater ability to overcome them. Therefore, nothing could replace its purpose. The softest will overcome the hardest. The weakest will overcome the strongest. Nobody in the world does not know this. Yet, nobody does practise it. Therefore, sages have a saying that states: *"Accept the country's shame and be called the Kingdom's leader. Accept the country's misfortune and be called the world's King."* True words seem to be paradoxical.

79

Calm a great hate and certainly some hate will remain. How could this be considered competent? Therefore, sages adhere to orthodox agreements and do not obligate other people by purpose. Therefore, those with virtue will uphold the agreement. Those without virtue will uphold the details. The Way of nature has no favourites. It is always with the competent people.

80

In a small country with a few people, let everybody have many tools, but not use them. Let the people be serious about death and not move far away. Let them have carriages without using them. Let them have weapons without displaying them. Let them return to knotted cords and use them. Sweeten their food and beautify their clothes. Enjoy their customs and secure their dwellings. Neighbouring countries will see each other in the distance. They hear each other's chickens and dogs. Nevertheless, the people die of old age and have never visited each other.

81

True words are not pleasing. Pleasing words are not true. Those who know are not educated. Those who are educated do not know. Those who are competent have not much. Those who have much are not competent. Sages do not hoard. Since they are used to act for other people, they receive more possessions for themselves. Since they are used to give to other people, they have much more themselves. Therefore, the Way of nature is beneficial and without harm. Accordingly, the Way of people should be action without strive.

Discussion

Congratulations, you have completed the first step of your 2,500 years journey back to the eternal wisdom of ancient China. You have almost reached your destiny. Almost—because *Lao Zi's Dao De Jing* contains still hidden layers of poetic beauty, wisdom, and knowledge. The aim of my book *Lao Zi's Dao De Jing: Meta-translation (Schade, 2016)[3]* was to create a reliable English version for the book that you are reading right now. Whether my attempt was successful or not, there are still many levels of understanding hidden within Lao Zi's manuscript. No matter how reliable, no translation is sufficient for an adequate understanding of Lao Zi. Even Chinese people reading a pristine copy of his manuscript in their mother language, need to discover the eternal wisdom that lays buried deep below the surface of Lao Zi's poetic style and simple words. In accord, Lao Zi warned his readers—*My words are very easy to understand and very easy to apply. Yet, people cannot understand them and they cannot apply them (70).* He also states that he does not intend to enlighten them—*Do not use the Way to enlighten people. Instead, use it to keep them simple. People are difficult to rule if they use their knowledge (65).* Furthermore, he created confusion by using a poetic-holistic style and different poetic names for the same concepts such as—*The Way, Nothing, One, Father, Mother, Valley Spirit, etc.*

---

[3] Appendix: Lao Zi Meta-translation

This suggests that *Lao Zi's Dao De Jing* is an esoteric manuscript that contains hidden knowledge about the *Way of Nature* and the *Way of People*.

To add to the confusion, *Lao Zi's Dao De Jing: Chinese-English Dictionary (Schade, 2017)*[4] shows that each Chinese pictograph has many meanings. The actual meaning of each pictograph is determined by its context, which is Lao Zi's sophisticated philosophy. In order to understand *Dao De Jing*, one needs to know the core of Lao Zi's philosophy. For two and halve thousand years, thousands of scholars around the world have tried to discover that key. Despite their great efforts, it remained hidden behind the poetic veil of Lao Zi's misleading simplicity.

My study suggests that the core of Lao Zi's brilliant philosophy is his sentence—*The One generated the Two (42)*. That has been the guiding principle for the explanations in my book—*Lao Zi's Dao De Jing Explained (Schade, 2017)*.[5] The ancient *Ma Wang Dui* texts are the most pristine versions of *Dao De Jing* available, because they were buried in an undisturbed tomb for over two thousand years. Intriguingly, compared to those texts, that crucial line was moved in later versions. That displacement of one single sentence increased the elusiveness of Lao Zi's manuscript significantly. Was this

---

[4] Appendix: Lao Zi Dictionary
[5] Appendix: Lao Zi Explained.

done to clarify the text, or alternatively, to hide the knowledge of a civilization that Lao Zi called the *'Ancients'*?

Think Smarter with Nemonik Thinking (Schade, 2016)[6] is the operating manual for your mind that you should have received at birth. Nemonik thinking is a smarter way of thinking that aims to maximize your success by evaluating seventeen nemoniks, which are memorized keywords describing all the perceived aspects of the mind, reality, and their interaction. In terms of Lao Zi's philosophy—*Success is to obtain what you seek and escape what you suffer (62)*. You might be the smartest thinker in the world, but only nemonik thinking could make you the smartest thinker you can be. Lao Zi's *Dao De Jing* is important for nemonik thinking, because it provides a rationale. In addition, it provides the eternal wisdom that is required to make productive decisions about each of the 17 nemoniks. Therefore, the nemonik template is used to reorganize Lao Zi's manuscript for *Lao Zi's Dao De Jing for Nemonik Thinkers (Schade, 2016).*[7]

---

[6] Appendix: Nemonik Thinking
[7] Appendix: Lao Zi for Nemonik Thinkers.

Appendices

Bibliography

Schade, A. (2016). *Lao Tzu's Tao Te Ching* (1 ed.). nemonik-thinking.org.

Schade, A. (2016). *Lao Zi's Dao De Jing for Nemonik Thinkers* (1 ed.).

Schade, A. (2016). *Lao Zi's Dao De Jing: Meta-translation* (1 ed.). nemonik-thinking.org.

Schade, A. (2016). *Think Smarter with Nemonik Thinking.* nemonik-thinking.org.

Schade, A. (planned 2017). *Lao Zi's Dao De Jing Explained* (1 ed.). nemonik-thinking.org.

Schade, A. (planned 2017). *Lao Zi's Dao De Jing: Chinese-English Dictionary* (1 ed.). nemonik-thinking.org.

Schade, A. (planned 2017). *Sun Zi's The Art of War* (1 ed.). nemonik-thinking.org.

Schade, A. (planned 2017). *The Unreal Reality* (1 ed.). nemonik-thinking.org.

My Other Books

Lao Zi's Dao De Jing

Lao Zi's Dao De Jing (Schade, 2016).

This book contains unique Chinese and English versions of Lao Zi's *Dao De Jing*, which means—*The Way of Nature and the Way of People.* Lao Zi was a Chinese philosopher who lived during the 6th century BC but is still ahead of our time. His brilliance outshines intellectual giants such as Confucius, Sun Zi, Socrates, Plato, and Aristotle. Lao Zi's aim is achieving success, which is to *obtain what you seek and escape what you suffer.* Success is achieved by aligning the *Way of People* with the *Way of Nature.* Lao Zi's success is secular and based on competence, rather than devotion. It is about positioning, rather than competing. Lao Zi's deep understanding of nature and people is crucial for your immediate survival and that of the next generation. Humanity is facing overpopulation, dwindling resources, nuclear warfare, pollution, climate change, etc. We cannot solve those problems with the same way of thinking that is causing them. The brutal reality shows that our way of thinking is failing. Therefore, Lao Zi's eternal wisdom is the guiding light for our future. Its simplicity reaches peacefully across the boundaries of race, religion, spiritualism, ideology, and science.

Lao Zi Meta-translation

Lao Zi's Dao De Jing: Meta-translation (Schade, 2016).

Lao Zi's eternal wisdom shines through in the numerous English translations of his *Dao De Jing*. Nevertheless, comparisons show that some individual Chinese pictographs and their interpretations are unclear. Therefore, this meta-translation is based on seven reputable Chinese versions. In order to select the most reliable pictographs, each one was compared across all versions. As changes might have occurred over time, the chance of a pictograph being included depended on the age of the version in which it appears. The consistent use of each pictograph was enhanced by computer assisted comparisons across the entire text. In addition, ten reputable English translations were synthesized in order to extract an initial context for each pictograph. The selected pictographs were translated with *Lao Zi's Dao De Jing: Chinese-English Dictionary (Schade, 2016)* that was compiled for this purpose. The guiding principle for this meta-translation has been the core of Lao Zi's philosophy—*The One generated the Two*. The importance of that sentence is explained in *Lao Zi's Dao De Jing Explained (Schade, 2017)*.

Lao Zi Explained

Lao Zi's Dao De Jing Explained (Schade, planned 2017).

For more than two and a half thousand years, *Dao De Jing* has been shrouded in mystery. The poetic beauty of Lao Zi's words has maintained its dazzling shine that hides his esoteric secrets. In accord, Lao Zi wrote—*My words are very easy to understand and very easy to apply. Yet, people cannot understand them and they cannot apply them.* Many scholars have attempted unsuccessfully to peel away layer after layer of meaning to unravel its cryptic secrets. In contrast, the present book reveals Lao Zi's secret teachings for the first time in a clearly understandable way, imparting hidden knowledge about the *Way of Nature* and the *Way of People.* The core of Lao Zi's teachings is success, which is—*obtaining what you seek and escaping what you suffer.* Success is secular and based on competence, rather than devotion. It is about positioning, rather than competing. It is achieved by aligning the *Way of People* with the *Way of Nature.* The guiding principle for the present explanation is the core of Lao Zi's philosophy—*The One generated the Two.* Humanity is facing huge manmade problems with a failing way of thinking. Therefore, Lao Zi's eternal wisdom is more relevant than ever.

Lao Zi for Nemonik Thinkers

Lao Zi's Dao De Jing for Nemonik Thinkers (Schade, 2016).

Lao Zi's Dao De Jing: Meta-translation (Schade, 2016) provides a reliable Chinese-English translation. Nevertheless, *Dao De Jing* has no rational sequence comprising an introduction, main body, and discussion. Even the division of the manuscript in the parts *Dao* and *De* is ambiguous. Topics concerning the *Way of Nature* and the *Way of People* appear almost ad random in the parts *Dao* and *De*. Similar to the notation *Jing*, the division in *Dao* and *De* might have been added later. Lao Zi's unfamiliar format suggests that he used a holistic, rather than a rational approach. He seems to walk around the topic, while telling the reader what he is seeing from different angles. Although that approach enhances the mystery and poetic beauty of that amazing manuscript, it did not produce the most efficient teaching tool. Therefore, I have used the nemonik template to restructure *Dao De Jing* for nemonik thinkers. This template was introduced in *Think Smarter with Nemonik Thinking (Schade, 2016)*.

Download a free eBook version
@ nemonik-thinking.org

Lao Zi Dictionary

Lao Zi's Dao De Jing: Chinese-English Dictionary (Schade, 2017).

Lao Zi's manuscript is more than 2,500 years old, while most Chinese-English dictionaries focus on the modern meaning of Chinese pictographs. Therefore, this special dictionary was compiled from several reputable public resources in order to get as close to the true meaning of each pictograph as possible. *Lao Zi's Dao De Jing: Meta-translation (Schade, 2016)* is based on seven Chinese versions of *Dao De Jing.* Altogether, those versions comprise about 1,600 different pictographs, which are included in the present dictionary. Furthermore, this dictionary introduces a unique numerical coding system for Chinese pictographs that could improve the search method concerning hard copies of Chinese reference books.

Download a free eBook version
@ nemonik-thinking.org

Nemonik Thinking

Think Smarter with Nemonik Thinking (Schade, 2016).

This is the operating manual for your mind that you should have received at birth. Nemonik thinking is a smarter way of thinking that aims to maximize your success by evaluating seventeen nemoniks, which are memorized keywords describing all the perceived aspects of your mind, reality, and their interaction. Success is obtaining what you seek and escaping what you suffer. To maximize that success, nemonik thinking mobilizes the hidden genius, accelerates thinking, improves memory, reveals opportunities and threats, creates questions and ideas, and reduces stress levels. It is like playing a musical keyboard with seventeen keys producing an infinite repertoire of smart strategies. Nemonik thinking is unique because it is the first exhaustive and transferable way of thinking. In contrast, conventional thinking is time consuming. Hence, the less time you have, the greater the necessity to study nemonik thinking. You might be the smartest thinker in the world, but only nemonik thinking could make you the smartest thinker you can be.

Download a free eBook version

@ nemonik-thinking.org

Nemonik Glossary

Glossary of Nemonik Thinking (Schade, 2016).

Nemonik thinking is a competitive advantage because it mobilizes the hidden genius, accelerates thinking, improves memory, prevents blind-spots, and reveals opportunities, while its constant preparedness reduces stress levels. Definitions, associated with the mind and reality, are inherently hypothetical, fuzzy, and intertwined. Nevertheless, to improve our understanding of the way we think, we have to identify, differentiate, and define those components. Therefore, this glossary provides descriptions for the concepts associated with nemonik thinking. To become skilled in nemonik thinking, it is recommended to study— *Think Smarter with Nemonik Thinking (Schade, 2016).*

Download a free eBook version
@ nemonik-thinking.org

Nemonik Dictionary

Dictionary Nemonik Thinking (Schade 2016).

Nemonik thinking mobilizes the hidden genius, accelerates thinking, improves memory, reveals opportunities and threats, creates questions and ideas, and reduces stress levels. Nemonik thinking divides the mind into 17 nemonik regions. That division defragments information, which facilitates the storage, maintenance, recall, and processing of associated information from memory. However, the boundaries of the nemonik regions are fuzzy. Therefore, the aim of this dictionary is to differentiate them by providing keywords for each nemonik concept. The first part of this dictionary translates nemonik concepts into common keywords e.g. *advance* into attack, bypass, etc. In contrast, the second part translates common keywords into nemonik concepts e.g. attack, bypass, etc. into *advance*. This dictionary shows that the complexity of conventional thinking comprises thousands of keywords that can be simplified to 17 nemoniks. This reduction will increase the speed of your thinking. To become skilled in nemonik thinking, it is recommended to study—*Think Smarter with Nemonik Thinking (Schade, 2016)*.

Education Kills Humanity

Education Kills Humanity (Schade, 2016).

Humanity is facing huge manmade problems such as overpopulation, dwindling resources, pollution, climate change, and warfare. Nevertheless, we should not blame corrupt politicians, uncaring industrialists, greedy investors, passionate greenies, and warmongers. They are the products of our educational system, which conditions students with ratings to maximize the probability of winning. Winning is defeating opponents in competition. Therefore, conventional thinking is conflict oriented, which fosters aggression, control, effort, and force. This inhibits the truth and, therefore, it is self-destructive. The educational failure is maintained by cognitive dissonance and groupthink. In contrast, nemonik thinking aims for success, which is to obtain what you seek and to escape what you suffer. Therefore, nemonik thinking is goal oriented, which fosters freedom, alignment, compassion, allies, and win-win strategies. You might be the smartest thinker in the world, but only nemonik thinking could make you the smartest thinker you can be. This manuscript is an abridged version of *Think Smarter with Nemonik Thinking (Schade, 2016).*

Global Warming

Global Warming is the Solution (Schade, 2016).

This book presents a bilateral hypothesis for climate change. Mainstream climatology lacks scientific integrity and statistical methodology. Peer review is changed into peer pressure and objectors are silenced by labelling them *'Deniers'*. Proper statistical analyses are replaced by fancy graphs and non-causal correlation analyses. The conclusions are predominantly based on the last 166 years, while 420,000 years of Antarctic data are ignored. Climatology also ignores the solar expert Professor Zharkova, who predicts a mini ice-age by 2030. The present study shows that the current 400 ppm of CO_2 predicts a global temperature of 11.5 °C. It also shows that the observed global temperature of 1.3 °C failed to reach statistical significance. In addition, the data support the hypothesis that we live in a glacial period. This hypothesis is supported by the thermal gap of CO_2, the long interglacial duration, and the interglacial thermal stability. Consequently, decreasing atmospheric CO_2 could induce glacial conditions threatening the survival of humanity.

Download a free eBook version

@ nemonik-thinking.org

Sun Zi's The Art of War

Sun Zi's The Art of War (Schade, planned 2017).

Sun Zi (554-496 BC) was a Chinese warrior-philosopher who wrote the military classic *Bing Fa* or *The Art of War*. Although his book is about war, his strategies apply to every facet of daily life. Sun Zi deals with the art of positioning yourself in space, matter, and time. He addresses the questions raised by nemonik thinking of where, what, and when to advance, stay, retreat, accumulate, preserve, dispose, act, wait, prepare, accept, reject, reveal, and conceal. Think smarter and incorporate Sun Zi's strategies in your thinking. To become skilled in nemonik thinking, it is recommended to study—*Think Smarter with Nemonik Thinking (Schade, 2016)*.

Download a free eBook version
@ nemonik-thinking.org

Website

It is the aim of my website to provide interactive on-line information about nemonik thinking. This includes discussions, books, blog, videos, exercises, updates, activities, web links, and tests. Join the nemonik thinkers and receive the latest updates. It is a work in progress. Check it out and have your say! I look forward to your feedback at:

nemonik-thinking.org

www.ingramcontent.com/pod-product-compliance
Lightning Source LLC
Chambersburg PA
CBHW070554030426
42337CB00016B/2488